IT'S FUN TO SPEAK
FRENCH

with

By Teresa Scibor

Illustrated by Richard Ollive

BARRON'S

One windy morning, Madame Bigoudi was hanging out her
wash in the yard.

"My goodness!" she said.

"Ça alors!" said the birds.

"It's Zozo!"

"C'est Zozo!"

"Oh, no. Stop! Stop!" she cried.

"Arrête! Arrête!" cried the birds.

But it was too late. Zozo had landed.

"Good morning, Madame Bigoudi," said Zozo.

"Bonjour, Madame," said Fleur, the flower.

And Moustache, the cat, smiled.

"Just look at that!" said Madame Bigoudi.

Regarde ça! said Fleur.

"I'm sorry, Madame," said Zozo.

Je suis désolée, echoed Fleur.

"Today we're going to the seaside," said Zozo.

Aujourd hui on va à la plage, smiled Fleur.

"Are the children ready?" asked Zozo.

"Ils sont prêts, les enfants?" said Fleur.

"Oh yes," replied Madame Bigoudi.

"Mais oui," said Fleur.

"Go and look for them. But be careful, Zozo!"

"Va les chercher. Mais attention, Zozo!"

But Zozo tripped.

"Ooooh! Ooops!" he cried.

"Zut alors!" cried Fleur.

Zozo whizzed past the living room and …

… shot straight into the kitchen.

"Ça alors!" said Monsieur Bigoudi who was making

pancakes.

"**Bonjour Zozo,**" he said. "Do you like pancakes?"

"**Tu aimes les crêpes?**" asked Fleur.

"Oh yes," said Zozo.

"**Mais oui,**" nodded Fleur.

"Look at this, Zozo!" said Monsieur Bigoudi.

"Regarde ça, Zozo!" said Fleur.

"One, two, three — up it goes and down it comes!"

"Un, deux, trois — hoplà et bah voilà!" sang Fleur.

"That's clever," said Zozo.

"C'est génial," agreed Fleur.

Zozo grabbed the frying pan.

"Let me try!"

"A moi! A moi!" cried Fleur. **"Un, deux, trois — hoplà et bah voilà!"** she sang.

"Oh, no!" said Zozo.

"Ah, non!" said Fleur.

"Oh, là là!" said Monsieur Bigoudi.

The pancake was stuck to the ceiling!

Just then, Madame Bigoudi came into the kitchen and something warm and soft plopped right on top of her head. It was the pancake.

"La crêpe!" gasped Fleur.

"Ah, non! Oh, là là!" cried Zozo and Fleur.

"Never mind, Zozo," comforted Monsieur Bigoudi as Madame

Bigoudi rushed out.

"Ne t'en fais pas," said Fleur.

"Where are the children?" asked Zozo.

"Où sont les enfants?" asked Fleur.

"Upstairs. Go and find them," said Monsieur Bigoudi.

"En haut. Va les chercher," said Fleur.

"All right," said Zozo running upstairs.

"D'accord," echoed Fleur.

Suddenly, Zozo was flying through the air and …

"Zozo! What *are* you doing?" shrieked Madame Bigoudi.

"Mais qu'est-ce que tu fais?" cried Fleur.

"I don't know!" spluttered Zozo.

"Je ne sais pas!" wept Fleur.

"I'm wet!" Zozo wailed.

"Je suis trempée!" said Fleur tearfully.

Just then, three heads peeked around the door.

"**Bonjour, Zozo,**" said Luc and Sophie cheerfully.

"**Salut Luc! Salut Sophie!**" answered Fleur.

And Rififi barked loudly and wagged his tail.

"You do look funny, Zozo!" exclaimed Sophie.

"**Tu es rigolo!**" giggled Fleur.

"What are you doing in there, Zozo? We're going swimming in the sea," said Luc.

"Qu'est-ce que tu fais là, Zozo? Nous allons nager dans la mer," cried Fleur.

"And now you need dry pants and a shirt," said Madame Bigoudi.

"Un pantalon et une chemise," agreed Fleur.

Zozo got out quickly and dripped into Madame Bigoudi's bedroom.

Suddenly, they all heard a buzzing noise.

"What's that?" asked Luc.

"Qu'est-ce que c'est?" said Fleur.

"A big, black fly!" said Zozo.

"Une grande mouche noire!" said Fleur.

Zozo grabbed the biggest bottle he could see.

He quickly sprayed the fly and chased it around the room.

"Shoo!" cried Zozo.

"Va t'en!" shouted Fleur.

With a loud buzz, the fly zoomed out of the window.

"Hooray for Zozo!" the children cried.

Bravo! Bravo! Vive Zozo!" they cheered.

"Zozo, that was my *best* perfume," said Madame Bigoudi.

"C'était mon parfum préféré," echoed Fleur.

"What?" cried Zozo.

"Comment?" said Fleur.

"I'm so sorry, Madame," Zozo sighed.

"Je suis vraiment désolée," said Fleur.

And Rififi licked Zozo's hand.

"I'm hungry," said Zozo suddenly.

"J'ai faim," said Fleur.

He pulled out a bunch of bananas.

"Les bananes!" smiled Fleur.

Zozo gave one banana to Sophie and one to Luc.

"Une pour toi et une pour toi," counted Fleur.

And then, Zozo sang his Banana Song.

"That's lovely!" the children cried.

"C'est chouette!" said Fleur.

"Now, where are the pails and shovels?" asked Zozo.

"Où sont les seaux et les pelles?" said Fleur.

"In the bedroom," said Sophie.

"Dans la chambre," said Fleur.

"Let's go then!" cried Zozo jumping up.

"Allons-y!" said Fleur.

"Here are the swimsuits and the red and yellow ball," said Luc.

"Voici les maillots de bain et le ballon rouge et jaune," said Fleur.

"Good," said Zozo.

"Très bien," said Fleur.

"Let's go!" said Zozo.

"Allons-y!" echoed Fleur.

They were all ready to go when, suddenly, they heard Madame
Bigoudi.

"Help! My ring has gone down the drain hole! Help! Help!"

"Au secours! Au secours!" cried Fleur.

Zozo sprang to the rescue.

"Where's my banana bag?" he said, looking down into the balloon basket.

"Où est mon sac-banane?" said Fleur.

"Here it is. I'm coming!" cried Zozo.

"Le voici! J'arrive!" cried Fleur.

"Let me try!" Zozo said.

"A moi! A moi!" said Fleur.

"Here's the fishing rod," said Moustache.

"Voici la canne," said Fleur.

"And here's the magic magnet," said Zozo.

"Et voici l'aimant magique," added Fleur.

"**Un, deux, trois,**" they all counted.

"And here's your ring, Madame," said Zozo.

"**Et voilà la bague, Madame,**" said Fleur.

"**Bravo, bravo! Vive Zozo!**" cheered the children.

"Thank you. Thank you very much," said Madame Bigoudi. She
kissed Zozo and handed him a big bunch of bananas.

"Merci. Merci beaucoup," echoed Fleur.

"And here's a package of potato chips for Moustache," she said.

"Les chips! Les chips!" said Fleur, looking longingly at the
package.

"Come on then, children!" said Zozo.

"We're off!"

"Allez, allez les enfants! On y va!" cried Fleur.

The children waved good-bye to Mommy and Daddy.

"Au revoir, Maman! Au revoir, Papa!"

Dans un ciel sans nuages,
Que c'est beau!
Nous allons à la plage,
Vive Zozo!
Nous sommes tous très contents,
Nous flottons dans le vent
à la plage!

The balloon went up and they were off to the seaside – **à la plage**.

And there, they felt sure, another exciting adventure was waiting for them.

Zozo's Special Words

Here are all the words and phrases in French and in English. Be sure to practice your pronunciation while listening to the tape.

ACTION WORDS

j'arrive	I'm on my way / I'm coming
nous allons à la plage	we're going to the seaside
nous allons nager	we're going swimming
nous flottons (dans le vent)	we're floating (in the wind)
qu'est-ce que tu fais?	what are you doing?

CLOTHES

une chemise	a shirt
les maillots de bain	the swimsuits
un pantalon	a pair of pants

COLORS

jaune	yellow
noire	black
rouge	red

COMMANDS

allez, allez les enfants!	let's go children!
allons-y!	let's go!
amusez-vous bien!	enjoy yourselves!
arrête!	stop!
attention!	be careful! / watch out!
ne t'en fais pas!	don't worry! / it doesn't matter!
on y va!	we're off!
regarde ça!	look at this! / that!
va les chercher!	go and find them!
va t'en!	go away!

DESCRIPTIVE WORDS

beau	beautiful
bonnes	good
contents	happy
grande	tall / big
petit	small
prêts	ready

EVERYDAY EXPRESSIONS

c'est chouette	that's lovely / super
c'est facile	it's easy
c'est génial	that's clever / terrific
c'est . . . Zozo	it's . . . Zozo
c'était mon parfum préféré	that was my best / favorite perfume
comment?	what? / I beg your pardon?
d'accord	all right / okay
hoplà et bah voilà	up it goes and down it comes
ils sont prêts, les enfants?	are the children ready?
j'adore ça	I love this / that / them
j'ai faim	I'm hungry

je ne sais pas	I don't know
je ne suis pas content	I'm not happy
je suis content	I'm happy
je suis désolée	I'm sorry
je suis vraiment désolée	I'm *so* sorry
je suis trempée	I'm soaked
mais non	of course not
merci (beaucoup)	thank you (very much)
miam! miam!	yum-yum!
non / ah, non	no / of course not / oh, no
nous sommes tous très contents	we're all very happy
on va . . . à la plage	we're off . . . to the seaside
où sont les enfants?	where are the children?
oui / mais oui	yes / yes, of course
qu'est-ce que c'est?	what's this? / what's that?
que c'est beau	how beautiful it is
tu aimes . . . les crêpes?	do you like . . . pancakes?
tu es rigolo	you're funny / you look funny
très bien	very good / very well

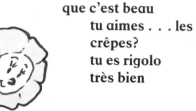

EXCLAMATIONS

à moi!	my turn!
au secours!	help!
bravo!	well done!
ça alors!	my goodness!
oh, là là!	oh, dear!
vive (Zozo)!	hooray (for Zozo)!
youpie!	hurrah!
zut alors!	oops!

FOOD

les bananes	the bananas
les chips	the potato chips
la crêpe	the pancake

GREETINGS AND FAREWELLS

à bientôt	see you soon
au revoir	good-bye
bonjour	good morning
salut	hello

NUMBERS

un	one
deux	two
trois	three

OBJECTS

l'aimant (magique)	the (magic) magnet
la bague	the ring
le ballon	the ball
la canne	the fishing rod
une mouche	a fly
le nuage	the cloud
le parfum	the perfume
les pelles	the shovels
le sac	the bag
les seaux	the pails
le vent	the wind